Postman Pat's
Friends

Scholastic Children's Books,
Commonwealth House, 1-19 New Oxford Street,
London WC1A 1NU, UK
a division of Scholastic Ltd

London ~ New York ~ Toronto ~ Sydney ~ Auckland

First published by Scholastic Ltd, 1997

Text copyright © Scholastic Ltd 1997
Transparencies copyright © Woodland Animations 1997

ISBN 0 590 19363 5

Printed in Belgium by Proost.

This is Postman Pat's wife Sara. She looks after their son, Julian.

Pat meets his friends Miss Hubbard and
Mrs Pottage.

Pat gives Mrs Pottage some letters.

Pat and Jess meet Katy Pottage who is out shopping with her mum.

Pat's old friend Granny Dryden is taking a ride on the Postbus.

This is Dr Gilbertson. She looks after the people of Greendale when they are sick.

Julian and his friends enjoy going on
nature walks with their teacher Mr Pringle.

Miss Hubbard and Ted Glen have a
friendly chat with Pat.

Pat often meets Sam Waldron with his mobile shop.

Alf Thompson is usually busy on his farm but sometimes he sees Pat in the village.

When Postman Pat delivers letters to the farm, he and Jess see Dorothy Thompson.

The twins, Tom and Katy Pottage, are best friends as well as brother and sister.

Sometimes when Pat and Jess are out delivering letters, Jess makes new friends!

Pat and Jess drive home thinking of all their friends in Greendale.